Read & Respo

Ages
7–11

Read & Respond

Ages 7–11

Author: Celia Warren

Development Editor: Marion Archer

Editor: Tracy Kewley

Assistant Editor: Margaret Eaton

Series Designer: Anna Oliwa

Designer: Liz Gilbert

Illustrations: Simon Walmesley

Text © 2011, Celia Warren © 2011, Scholastic Ltd

Designed using Adobe InDesign

Published by Scholastic Ltd,
Book End, Range Road, Witney,
Oxfordshire OX29 0YD
www.scholastic.co.uk

Printed by Bell & Bain
1 2 3 4 5 6 7 8 9   1 2 3 4 5 6 7 8 9 0

British Library Cataloguing-in-Publication Data
A catalogue record for this book is available from
the British Library.
ISBN 978-1407-12624-1

Acknowledgements
The publishers gratefully acknowledge permission to reproduce the
following copyright material: **David Higham** for the use of extracts from
The Hundred-Mile-An-Hour Dog by Jeremy Strong. Text © 1996, Jeremy
Strong (1996, Viking); **Puffin Books** for use of illustrations by Nick
Sharratt and the front cover from *The Hundred-Mile-An-Hour Dog* by
Jeremy Strong. Illustrations © 1996, Nick Sharratt (1996, Viking). Every
effort has been made to trace copyright holders for the works reproduced
in this book, and the publishers apologise for any inadvertent omissions.

The Hundred-Mile-An-Hour Dog

About the book

Jeremy Strong's inimitable humour is alive and kicking in *The Hundred-Mile-An-Hour Dog*: 12 chapters of hilarity, just the right side of plausible, that allow readers to romp willingly through the ups and downs of life with Streaker, who is part greyhound, part Ferrari and part whirlwind. A bribe from Trevor's mother to walk the uncontrollable Streaker throughout the Easter school holidays prompts the boy, and his best friend, Tina, to think of a series of ways to try to train the dog. Each scenario is wilder than the last, and Trevor ends up at the police-station more than once. The friends' efforts are hindered by the malevolent bully, Charlie Smugg, son of police officer Sergeant Smugg (who, Trevor's dad knows, cheats at golf). There is an unspoken animosity between the two families, and when the police-officer threatens to see that Streaker is put down, Trevor's family all pull together to protect their dog. Eventually, it is Trevor's final invention during another attempt to train Streaker, that (almost literally) backfires but then succeeds in the task. Streaker becomes obedient by default and her life is saved. At the same time, Trevor and Tina are spared a dunking in a bath full of filthy water and frogspawn, at the hands of Charlie, and secure the promised £30 reward for walking the dog.

Children with a sense of humour will love this story, and will doubtless relate to parents' preoccupations that have no bearing on their own lives, beyond offering glimpses of humorous incomprehension: Mum's efforts to slim; Dad's obsession with golf. The story offers huge page-turning incentives and contains laugh-out-loud descriptions, made funnier through the narrator's tendency towards exaggeration and irony. Realistic dialogue, graphic descriptions and strongly rounded characters help the children to feel as if they belong to this family, and share its hopes and fears. At the same time, the story opens up talking points, not least on ways of dealing with everyday issues and stresses with perseverance, optimism, cheerfulness, determination, loyalty and, of course, humour.

About the author

On Jeremy Strong's website (www.jeremystrong.co.uk) the author talks about his writing in an interview with Streaker (his character). He says, 'I like writing funny stories. I did try to write a really serious story once but it made me miserable and I started putting in jokes to cheer myself up. Of course in the end it turned into another funny story.' Fans will be very pleased it did. His light-touch humour is his hallmark.

Jeremy Strong had a 30-year marriage that resulted in two (now grown-up) children, after which he and his wife parted, and he remarried. After university, he became a primary teacher and headteacher but has been writing full-time for the past 20 years. He visits schools worldwide. Jeremy Strong has written around 80 children's books. His story, *There's a Viking in my Bed*, was developed into a BBC Children's TV series.

Facts and figures

First published in 1996 by Viking.
The Hundred-Mile-An-Hour Dog was overall winner of the Red House Children's Book Award, 1997.
In 2008, *Lost! The Hundred-Mile-An-Hour Dog*, was shortlisted for the Blue Peter Book Award for the 'Most Fun Story with Pictures'.

Guided reading

Before reading

Tell the children the title of the book and observe their reaction. Does the title make them smile? Can they tell you why? What are their expectations of the story? Discuss the concept of exaggeration and why people exaggerate (for effect, drama, to grab attention). Show the cover and the introductory words *Laugh your socks off with Jeremy Strong*. What does this indicate about the author's reputation? (He writes humorous books.)

Read the blurb on the back. Discuss how the metaphor *a rocket on four legs with a woof attached* indicates the author's style of humour. Draw attention to how the mention of *frogspawn* and *something very, very yucky* intrigues the reader, without giving away too much.

Chapter 1

Examine how Streaker's name, the first word of the whole story, reinforces the title and blurb, as well as establishing the focus of the story and Streaker as the main character. Explain that *0 to 100 mph* is the dog's supposed rate of acceleration. Ask in what context this expression usually occurs (cars' acceleration rate) and how long *the blink of an eye* is. Note how the first-person narrator, Trevor, is using exaggeration akin to the title of the book.

Ensure that the children understand, or discern from context, the meanings of *refuses… point-blank* (refuses bluntly, directly, with no room for manoeuvre), *twigged* (realised, recognised) and *the big crunch* (sticking point, tricky bit). Discuss how Mum's free-wheeling graphically presents her paying attention to her son's attempt at bargaining terms.

Can the children find examples of the narrator's chatty tone of voice, directly addressing the reader? (For example, *See? I'm not stupid*.) Discuss how this involves the readers, making them sympathetic to his situation.

Chapter 2

Discuss why the author chooses to digress from the plot at the beginning of this chapter. Can the children find which sentence links the opening description to Trevor's *BRILLIANT PLAN*? (*So what has all this got to do with Streaker?*) Comment on the use of capitals in places – used to add significance to a situation or event. Explain any words that the children do not know, for example *bazooka* (the onomatopoeic name of an anti-tank gun), *jammy* (crafty, cunning) and *Mach one* (a measure of aircraft speed, equal to the speed of sound).

Comment on the imagery, in the metaphors: *the bowels of my wardrobe, switched to turbo-boost* and simile: *like jet-trails*. Draw attention to the use of unusual, graphic verbs: *churned away, careering, lurched, tumbling* and so on. Point out how they make the description vivid and imaginable. Ask: *What is the effect of the short, sharp dialogue at the end of the descriptive passage – 'Stop that boy!'?* (It suggests that the boy and the dog are about to be stopped in their tracks, perhaps.)

Discuss the word-play in *old bag's lady* and the use of *Smugg* as the police officer's name. Talk about how readers are influenced in their opinion of Sergeant Smugg through his *laughing silently* and the reference to his cheating at golf. Note how a person's title, for example 'Mr' or 'Sergeant', is of most importance to the owner. Discuss if and why the children think that Trevor's dad deliberately called him Mr Smugg, rather than Sergeant Smugg. (Indicates a lack of respect.)

Invite the children to compare *Streaker proceeded to give Dad's ears a good clean-out* with, for example, 'began to lick Dad's ears'. Ask: *Why is the author's description funnier?* (Sounds as though the dog has a set intention; as if it's for Dad's own good rather than the dog simply misbehaving.) Note how the chapter ends on an appetite-whetting note, with the promise of meeting a new character.

Guided reading

Chapter 3

Look at the use of capitals to stress the 'Shock! Horror!' factor of *HIS BEST FRIEND'S A GIRL!* Note how the narrator gives physical descriptions of himself and Tina in a conversational way, revealing that each is self-conscious about their own appearance (for example, he is *small and weedy*; she has *loads of freckles*).

Discuss why Trevor might choose *Ninety-nine per cent fat-free yoghurt* as a funny order for Tina's dog to ignore (words he would read and hear a lot, as his mother is dieting). Remind the children how Streaker's name reflects her behaviour literally; introduce the term irony, and the ironic use of Mouse as the opposite of the real size of Tina's dog. Consider, too, the ironic verbs used: *visited* (gardens) and *used* (an old lady). Ask the children if they recognise the original source of the paraphrased quotation *Was it a bird? Was it a plane?* (From *Superman*.)

Chapter 4

Compare the opening words of this chapter with those of the previous one and note how they both address the reader. Had the children guessed the relationship between the Smuggs? This chapter, again, is full of graphic similes – *arms like King Kong, like an asthmatic donkey, like a cruise missile*. Talk about how and why the similes work well (they are extended, exaggerated, unusual). Highlight the references in the description of Charlie Smugg to prehistoric man and the fictitious characters King Kong and Quasimodo, and discuss what features the references have in common. (All unflattering in terms of appearance and/or behaviour.) Comment on the rhetorical nature of the closing question.

Chapter 5

Talk about the meaning of *Behaviour Modification* and discuss what less 'politically correct' words could be used instead of 'modification' (improvement, correction). Point out how using words such as 'modify' rather than 'improve' or 'correct' avoids suggesting value-judgements.

Challenge the children to identify further examples of exaggeration and irony, such as the dog's stomach becoming *the size of a hot-air balloon*, arms… *half a mile long*, and the irony of *This was brilliant progress*. Discuss the children's use of bribery on Streaker, and how it compares to Mum's bribery of Trevor.

Chapter 6

Read aloud *Killer Sludge from Planet Sqwirkkk* and comment on the spelling and the concept. Discuss how far the character's sense of humour reflects the author's, who puts the words into the narrator's mouth. By describing the clump of nettles as *the only clump of nettles in the world that needed a set of traffic lights*, to what is the narrator comparing the dogs? (Traffic.) Note how this is an implied simile rather than a direct one.

Chapter 7

Consider how each successive episode develops the relationship between Trevor and Tina, and discuss what they have in common, why they get on well, and how their thinking and actions complement each other. Talk about the word *ranks* (*of glittering teeth*) and the images it conjures up (soldiers, shiny armour, weapons, helmets, aggressive, warlike).

Can the children spot more rhetorical questions at the end of this chapter and the opening of the next? Ask: *Which one is ironic?* (*Isn't life wonderful?*)

Chapter 8

Draw attention to the increasing font size and change to capitals of the word *on*. Ask the children which word on the following page describes

Guided reading

someone going on and on (*rant*). Can they infer the meaning of *rave*? Talk about why Trevor thought better than to share his thoughts with his angry parents. Ask: *How would his parents see such comments?* (As impertinent, cheeky, adding insult to injury, belying his saying sorry.) Identify where the narrative digresses from the plot. (Trevor's idea of harnessing Dad's *explosions* to power electricity.) Ask: *What do these asides contribute to the book?* (Humour for the reader, and indications of how Trevor's mind works: how he uses such thoughts to diffuse his father's anger.) What can readers infer from the fact that Charlie Smugg *pushed past* after he had *plonked* Trevor down? Does the action imply Charlie's contempt for Trevor?

Chapter 9

By now, children should be quick to spot Trevor's use of exaggeration (*She had half a mile of tongue hanging out*). How many verbs can they spot that mean 'rushed' (*raced, hurtled, zoomed, charging*), and that mean 'shouted' (*yelled, bellowed*)? Talk about which of these verbs are onomatopoeic. Ask the children why they think Dad's attitude changes in this chapter. Did Sergeant Smugg cause the problem by provocation? How fairly does his saying of Streaker *She tried to eat my head!* represent the facts? How does this influence the reader's sympathies?

Chapter 10

How far do the children agree with the opening statement? (*It was weird.*) Can they explain why? Ask: *What does Trevor mean by a ray of hope?* What do the children think of each successive idea for training Streaker – are they getting more far-fetched and fantastic? And funnier? Ask the children if any of them know what the Tour de France is. (A major international cycling race.) Discuss the closing words: *The moment had come.* How do they encourage people to keep reading?

Chapter 11

Invite the children to imagine the speed with which this latest experiment happens – faster than it takes to read or write. Stop to picture the scene through Streaker's eyes – one minute she is fast asleep, then suddenly she hears the trigger-word *Walkies!*, and is shot from a strange contraption into the washing machine. Draw attention to the graphic verbs: *hurled, whizzed, rocketed, rammed.* Ask the children why the verb *toddle* is humorous, in relation to the fire-brigade. Who or what usually toddles? (Young children.) What effect does using an inappropriate verb have? (Humour, through minimalising the event.)

Discuss Tina's motivation in accepting responsibility for this experiment and her questions about their friendship. Is she being possessive, for example, or does she want Trevor to appreciate their friendship more?

Chapter 12

Ask the children what the word *Walkies* usually triggers in a dog's mind. Talk about how and why it now works differently with Streaker. Discuss why Trevor didn't want to tease Charlie about his girlfriend and how his behaviour differs from Charlie's. What do the children think was going through Tina's mind when she leaned towards Trevor? What made him run?

Shared reading

Extract 1

- Display and read Extract 1 after reading it in context in Chapter 2. Can the children remember how Trevor was travelling? (On roller skates, while hanging on to Streaker's lead.)
- Underline the graphic verbs: *scattering, zigzagged, careering, swerved, fling, screaming, lurched, tumbling, spilling, bounced, whizzed, smashed, hauled, clutching*. Invite the children to read them quickly as a list as you point to each in turn. Ask what effect these verbs have on the description. (Speeds up the action, imitates swift movement, emphasises the diversity of direction through the diversity of vocabulary.)

- Circle *Streaker was really enjoying herself*. Discuss why, finding evidence from the text. (*There's nothing she likes more than a good chase…*) Ask how Trevor might be feeling. Would his feelings change as he progressed through the market? How?
- Return to the opening words of the extract and draw attention to how the metaphorical phrase *hit the market* takes on a literal meaning retrospectively.
- Ask the children: *How does the closing sentence make Trevor sound like a model?* If necessary, explain *fetchingly*. (Attractively.)

Extract 2

- Read Extract 2 with the class and invite the children to compare Tina's and Trevor's reactions to the events as they occur. In what way does Tina's sense of humour match Trevor's? (Dry remarks, use of irony: *It may have been the cat, but I think it was your Dad's mobile phone…*)
- Talk about how Tina supports Trevor even though she hesitates. What does this suggest about their friendship?
- What can the children infer from the colours of the tufts of fur? Was the fight one-sided or was Streaker giving as good as she got?
- Circle the word *helpfully* and ask which word

follows that shows the word is used ironically. (*Useless.*)
- Mention the commonly used metaphor: 'my heart sank'. Underline the similar, extended metaphor used by Trevor (*My heart dive-bombed…*) Point out how adding sound to the image makes it funnier.
- Talk about the connotations of *Round Three*. (Fighting for sport, maybe boxing or wrestling.) In what way was the event *an emergency* in Trevor's eyes? What does he mean by *a hospital case*? (His dad might beat him.) Ask: *Is this another example of exaggeration?*

Extract 3

- Underline the opening three words. Note how a pronoun is used before the context is explained.
- Can the children rephrase *a pain*? (Nuisance, annoying or difficult.)
- Circle the words *predicament, pandemonium* and *inevitable* and invite the children to define them. (Plight, difficulty; chaotic confusion; inescapable, unavoidable.)
- Circle the verb *slinking*. Talk about why this is a good choice. Invite two children to demonstrate walking and slinking side by side, encouraging

the latter to look nervous, watchful and furtive, perhaps stooping their shoulders.
- Underline *ray of hope*. What sort of metaphor is this that makes it funny when Trevor goes on to say, *Actually… it was a small heap of junk…*? Explain that the metaphor is intangible, abstract.
- Talk about the reason for using capital letters in *AMAZINGLY BRILLIANT idea*, how it indicates the importance and impact of Trevor's idea, as far as he (and the plot) is concerned.

Extract 1

We hit the market at maximum speed, scattering shoppers in every direction. I held on for dear life as we zigzagged through the startled crowd, careering wildly from one side to the other. It was all I could do to stay upright.

Streaker suddenly swerved violently to one side to avoid a mesmerized old lady. I had to fling out one arm as a counter-balance and somehow I managed to get her handbag stuck on it.

'Help! I've been robbed! Stop that boy! He's taken my bag!'

In no time at all the whole market seemed to be after me, but there was no way I could stop and explain. Streaker was really enjoying herself. There's nothing she likes more than a good chase. She doesn't even care if she's chasing or being chased. We went screaming round corners so fast that my skates started to smoke. We lurched into stalls, sending them tumbling over and spilling their contents every which way, crashed into people and bounced off them, and all the time the crowd behind was getting bigger and bigger and noisier and noisier.

'Stop that boy!'

'He's stolen an old bag's lady – I mean an old lady's bag!'

'Get the bag-snatcher!'

Streaker whizzed round the next corner so fast that she rolled over and over, and of course I just carried straight on and smashed headlong into a rack of dresses. Before I knew it I was hauled to my feet by a very angry mob. Not only was I still clutching the old lady's handbag, but I had a rather stunning flower-print sun-dress draped fetchingly over one shoulder.

Text © 1996, Jeremy Strong.

Extract 2

Streaker turned and – this was quite astonishing really – made a single flying leap from the front doorstep and straight through an open window. The cat plunged after her and in no time at all a fight had broken out inside. I started praying silently: *please don't let anything happen to Dad's phone.* Tina peered desperately through the window while I banged on the front door.

'What's happening?' I shouted, still thumping away with my fists and getting no answer.

'I don't know. I saw something large fly through the air. It may have been the cat, but I think it was your Dad's mobile phone being a bit too mobile.'

That was it. I had to do something. Pushing Tina away, I saw Streaker and the cat go skidding out of the room. I started clambering through the window. 'I've got to get her.'

'Supposing somebody comes?' Tina asked anxiously.

'They're all out. I've got to get Dad's phone back before it's completely smashed.'

Tina only hesitated a fraction longer. 'I'm coming too,' she said and hopped in behind me.

There were quite a few tufts of fur lying around on the carpet, some black and some ginger. I found a bit of plastic and my heart dive-bombed into my boots and hid there squealing with terror.

'There's another bit over here,' Tina called out helpfully, picking up a large but useless lump of ex-mobile phone. 'At least it wasn't the cat,' she added.

To find Streaker all we had to do was follow the noise. The two animals seemed to have started Round Three upstairs. It was a bit spooky creeping around somebody else's house, but I hardly had time to think about it. This was an emergency. If Dad's phone was beyond repair, then I was going to end up a hospital case.

Text © 1996, Jeremy Strong

Extract 3

It was weird. Now that Streaker was under sentence of death everyone became very fond and protective of her. She had always been a pain, but she was also so bouncy and cheerful and, well . . . mad, and we loved her for it really. We didn't want to lose her. Mum and Dad spoke to her nicely and her predicament united us as a family. We fumed about the unfairness of it all and I wondered if there was a European Court of Doggy Rights. Dad even gave her extra meals. It didn't change the way she behaved, of course. She was still pandemonium with four legs, a tail, and a woof attached.

We were all very worried about her. I was scared to take her outside. I thought that Sergeant Smugg, or Charlie, or their Alsatians might pounce on us at any moment. Tina and I both felt pretty depressed. The holiday was almost over and it seemed inevitable that we would either get arrested or shoved in a bath full of frog-spawn and other assorted gunge. We couldn't win. However, Streaker had to go out sometimes and we went slinking up to the field in the evenings, hoping to avoid the Smuggs.

Then, two days before the end of the holiday, I discovered a ray of hope in the field. Actually, it wasn't exactly a ray of hope, it was a small heap of junk that somebody had dumped at the edge of the field. There was some old stair-carpet, bits of wood and some metal cylinders. I've no idea what the cylinders had been used for, but as soon as I saw them I got the most AMAZINGLY BRILLIANT idea ever. I grabbed Tina by the shoulder and stopped her.

'It's OK!' I shouted. 'We shall never have to walk Streaker again!'

Text © 1996, Jeremy Strong.

Plot, character and setting

Feeding the imagination

Objective: To interrogate text to deepen and clarify understanding and response.
What you need: Copies of *The Hundred-Mile-An-Hour Dog* and an enlarged copy of Extract 1 (page 8).

What to do
● Read Extract 1 together and discuss the setting. Ask: *Would the scene be as comical if Trevor and Streaker were racing through empty streets? Why not?*
● Discuss why the word *hit* in the opening sentence is an excellent choice, comparing its colloquial and literal meanings.
● Underline the term *counter-balance*. Invite two or three children to stand on one leg and then lean over as far as they can without falling over. Ask the rest of the class to observe what happens to their arms. Do they raise them to keep balance? Explain that their raised arms 'counter-balance' their raised legs. Note how the writer's attention to detail makes the scene more plausible. Challenge the children to look *mesmerized*, as if in a trance.
● Ask where else detail adds humour, for example, why say a *rather stunning flower-print sun-dress* rather than just 'a dress'? Examine each component of the phrase, noting how each detail increases the incongruity and humour.

Differentiation
For older/more confident learners: Invite the children to rewrite the passage, drawing on the senses and adding more humour where possible.
For younger/less confident learners: Encourage the children to discuss how well Nick Sharratt's drawing illustrates the text. Which sentences are shown in the picture? Can they draw their own version?

The value of dialogue

Objective: To explore how different texts appeal to readers using varied sentence structures and descriptive language.
What you need: Copies of *The Hundred-Mile-An-Hour Dog*, an enlarged copy of Extract 2 (page 9), photocopiable page 15 and writing materials.

What to do
● Display an enlarged copy of Extract 2 and read it together.
● Note how, here, the story is mostly carried through dialogue. Obscure the parentheses in the opening sentence and read aloud the simple sentence. Explain how the two dashes serve a similar purpose to brackets or commas. Discuss the advantage of adding this observation mid-sentence. (Helps the reader to 'see' things as they happen, and share the narrator's astonishment.)
● Ask what visual effect dialogue has on the layout. (The inset paragraphs for each fresh speech break the text into smaller 'bites'.)
● Ask how dialogue can encourage readers to read between the lines through inference. Explain that dialogue enables the author to 'show' rather than 'tell' what is happening. It also reveals characters' thoughts, and reasons for their behaviour, such as Trevor's feeling of urgency (*'I've got to get her.'*).
● Hand out photocopiable page 15, which asks the children to take a closer look at the use of dialogue, and what can be inferred from the dialogue, in Extract 2.

Differentiation
For older/more confident learners: Ask the children to continue the table on the back of their sheet, adding further direct speech quotations alongside their inference, starting with: *Well done, Tina... Nice one.*
For younger/less confident learners: Allow the children to work in groups and have an adult act as scribe, overseeing their discussion. Photocopy the completed table, create copies and cut out quotations and responses for the children to sort into pairs.

Plot, character and setting

Before and after

> **Objective:** To deduce characters' behaviour from their actions.
> **What you need:** Copies of *The Hundred-Mile-An-Hour Dog,* an enlarged copy of Extract 3 (page 10) and writing materials.

What to do

● Remind the children that the narrator writes in the first person. Display an enlarged copy of Extract 3 and read it together. How many sentences beginning with *I* can the children find in one minute?
● Ask what other first-person pronoun is used in this extract. Circle each use of *we*.
● Talk about how Trevor's approach to his task changes. Ask: *What is meant by Streaker's sentence of death? Is her life really at risk?*
● Discuss how Trevor's parents' attitude changes. Return to Chapter 1 and talk about his parents'

preoccupations (Mum's exercise and diet regime; Dad's golf obsession). Note the *strange squeak* that Mum gives when Trevor accepts her bribe. Ask: *What feelings does it reveal?* (Relieved, pleased.) *How differently does she feel now?* (Worried.)
● Identify the phrase that sums up the effect of the situation on the family (*...her predicament united us...*).

> **Differentiation**
> **For older/more confident learners:** Ask the children to create a table with two columns 'before' and 'after', with regard to Streaker's 'death sentence'. Provide time to fill in the columns with comments on the characters' changed behaviour, for example Trevor willing to walk Streaker/afraid to take her out; Dad blaming Trevor/blaming Smugg.
> **For younger/less confident learners:** Ask the children to explain in a short paragraph why the family members are worried and why Streaker's behaviour does not change.

The voice behind the narrator

> **Objective:** To infer the writer's perspective from what is written and from what is implied.
> **What you need:** Copies of *The Hundred-Mile-An-Hour Dog* and writing materials.

What to do

● Read the opening line in Chapter 9. Explain that the pronoun *one* refers to the previous chapter (Tina's idea). Ask: *What does the opening line suggest about the author's expectations?* (Curiosity will have made readers carry on.) *How does the author achieve a page-turning ending to Chapter 8?* (He closes with an intriguing question.)
● For both Trevor and Tina create a class list of the child characters' basic personality traits. Ask the children to support their deductions. (For example: Tina is loyal, optimistic and confident; she sticks by Trevor and doesn't let him give up.)
● Ask the children what the author's writing tells readers about his knowledge of human nature, by

looking at all the characters' behaviour. (Families pull together in a crisis; parents can seem preoccupied with their own interests.) Explain that this 'roundness of character' enables readers to imagine their personalities and behaviour even beyond the story.

> **Differentiation**
> **For older/more confident learners:** Challenge the children to list more generalities about human nature that are revealed in the story, adding textual support. (Some people are dishonourable – Charlie cheats; others are naturally considerate – Trevor doesn't want to gossip about Charlie.)
> **For younger/less confident learners:** Present to the children hypotheses about the child characters' relationship, such as: *Imagine Tina breaks her leg* or *What if Trevor was stuck on homework?* Then allow the children to discuss how the character's friend would respond. Explain how this reflects the roundness of the characters.

Plot, character and setting

Metaphors and similes

Objective: To explain how writers use figurative and expressive language to create images and atmosphere.
What you need: Copies of *The Hundred-Mile-An-Hour Dog,* writing materials, scissors and photocopiable page 16.

What to do
● From Chapter 10, read the following quotation: *She had always been a pain, but she was also so bouncy and cheerful and, well … mad, and we loved her for it really.*
● Ask: *Who is Trevor talking about?* (Streaker.) How can the children tell it is the dog? Can they think of any events that show these aspects of behaviour? For example, Streaker is disobedient – she ignores the 'sit' command and races off; she is friendly – she leaps into Trevor's dad's lap.
● Explain that these are factual statements; they are literal, not figurative. Tell the children that they are going to look for figurative descriptions of the dog – where metaphor or simile is used.
● Hand out photocopiable page 16 and ask the children to cut out and sort the quotations into metaphors and similes. Point out that there is one literal description among the quotations. Can they spot this?
● Bring everyone together to discuss how 'colourful' figurative language strengthens the reader's mental image.

Differentiation
For older/more confident learners: Alongside each quotation, ask the children to list adjectives describing what aspect of Streaker's behaviour is portrayed, for example *a large chunk of whirlwind* – fast, wild, bouncy.
For younger/less confident learners: Prompt the children to look for the words 'like' or 'as' when identifying similes, and 'is' or 'was' for metaphors.

A hundred-million exaggerations

Objective: To identify features that writers use to provoke readers' reactions.
What you need: Copies of *The Hundred-Mile-An-Hour Dog* and writing materials.

What to do
● When the children have read and enjoyed the whole book, invite them to describe its title. Prompt with questions such as: *Can any dog really run at 100mph?* Encourage the children to use the word 'exaggeration'.
● Divide the class into six groups. Appoint a scribe and spokesperson, and allocate two chapters to each group. Give the children a few minutes to scan the text and note all the examples of exaggeration that they can find. For example, in Chapter 1: *Streaker can out-accelerate a torpedo.*
● Invite each group to share two or three favourite examples and explain why they enjoyed them.

Discuss what and how this device adds to the narrative. (Adds humour, paints vivid pictures, adds emphasis, makes the text lively.)
● Challenge individuals to tell the class about something they did that morning, but using exaggeration, for example: *I ate a mountain of toast, spread with Spain's entire orange harvest.*
● Encourage the children to share their reactions to the examples. Ask: *Is it different in a story context from in real life?* (The former is more humorous; the latter renders suspicion over the speaker's account.)

Differentiation
For older/more confident learners: Challenge the children to invent chapter titles that use exaggeration, drawn from the events in each chapter.
For younger/less confident learners: Limit searches to one allocated chapter and give the children sticky paper markers to tag quotations.

Plot, character and setting

No gains without pains

Objective: To infer characters' feelings in fiction and consequences in logical explanations.
What you need: Copies of *The Hundred-Mile-An-Hour Dog*, photocopiable page 17 and writing materials.

What to do

● Talk about what persuades Trevor to let himself in for two weeks of walking an out-of-control dog. (Bribery: promise of £30.)
● Ask: *When Trevor's first plan fails, what inspires him to keep coming up with more ideas?* (Fear of losing the money and being dunked in filthy water.) *What does this reveal about his character?* (Determined? Foolish? Doesn't easily give up? Enjoys a challenge? Optimistic? Afraid?)
● Hand out photocopiable page 17. Ask the children to consider their responses and complete the sheet with reference to the text.
● Bring the class together to discuss their thoughts. Talk about Trevor's feelings at the outcome of each experiment. Ask: *Why might Tina feel more optimistic than Trevor?* (She is distanced from the situation as Streaker's not her dog, and she won't be in trouble with her parents. She has nothing to lose.)

Differentiation
For older/more confident learners: Challenge the children to write, for each experiment, what Trevor might have done differently in order to achieve a better outcome. (For example: 1. Avoid the market.)
For younger/less confident learners: Invite the children to work in twos or small groups, discussing each situation on the photocopiable sheet.

Storyboards

Objective: To identify and make notes of the main points of sections of texts.
What you need: Copies of *The Hundred-Mile-An-Hour Dog*, writing materials and photocopiable page 18.

What to do

● Invite the children to imagine they were watching *The Hundred-Mile-An-Hour Dog* as a television drama that was broadcast in several episodes. (Check that the children understand the word 'episode'.)
● Together briefly note down what might happen in Episode 1. Ask: *How many chapters would work well together? Where would it end? How would the producer ensure viewers would watch the next episode?*
● Explain that before such decisions are made, script-writers and producers need to summarise each chapter or event in sequence.
● Hand out photocopiable page 18 and ask the children to storyboard the book, keeping pictures simple (for example, they can draw stick-figures, colour-coded for the different characters).
● Encourage them to decide how to divide the story and note the action for each episode, adding a simple picture. Point out that they need not write full sentences. (The children may decide that they need more or fewer episodes, and can turn the page if necessary.)

Differentiation
For older/more confident learners: Challenge the children to choose one of the episodes they have written about and to expand their notes to show how the episode would be presented. For example, they might choose to show a flashback of Trevor watching a film about tanks.
For younger/less confident learners: Allow the children to work in twos, discussing where appropriate episode breaks might occur. Help them use bookmarks to divide the story before beginning to write notes.

SECTION
4

The value of dialogue

● Read the statements below. Tick the four that support the quotation.

> **"Dialogue in a story can be very useful."**

Dialogue:

…stops the story from getting boring by breaking up the narrative ☐

…moves the plot along without too much description ☐

…shows what characters are thinking ☐

…gives the author a chance to use speech marks ☐

…helps the author to show more than one viewpoint ☐

● Read Extract 2 and then complete the gaps in the table. You will either need to explain what you infer from the dialogue, or write the words from the text that imply what is suggested. An example has been completed for you.

Dialogue from Extract 2	What I infer from the speech
'What's happening?'	Trevor can't see through the window from the front door.
'Supposing somebody comes?'	
	Tina doesn't want to miss out on the adventure and wants to help.
	Trevor cares more about his Dad's phone than the animals' welfare.
'At least it wasn't the cat.'	
	Trevor believes the longer Streaker and the cat are fighting, the more likely his dad's phone will be broken.

● Explain how the descriptive paragraphs balance and support the dialogue.

_____

_____

_____

Text © 1996, Jeremy Strong.

SECTION
4

Metaphors and similes

● Read and cut out the quotations below. They are all about Streaker.
Sort the quotations into metaphors and similes.

● WARNING: One quotation is not figurative, it is a literal description.
Can you spot which one is neither a metaphor nor a simile? Identify this
quotation and label it 'Literal description'.

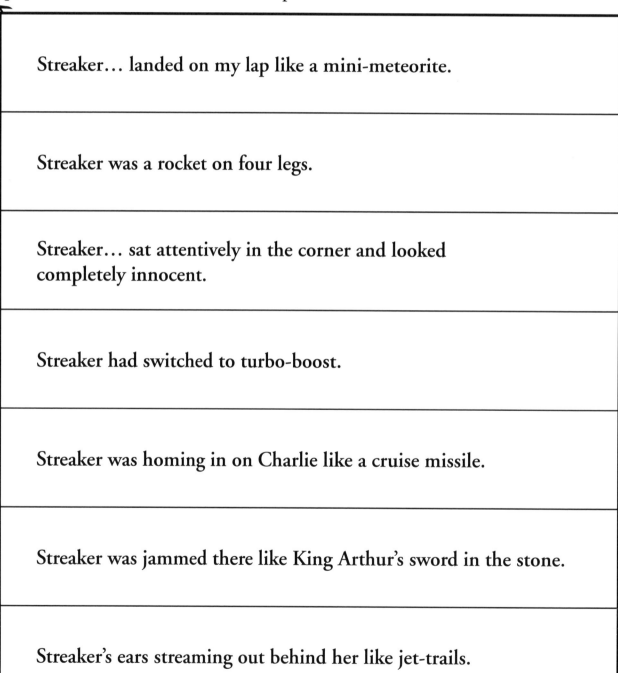

Streaker… landed on my lap like a mini-meteorite.

Streaker was a rocket on four legs.

Streaker… sat attentively in the corner and looked completely innocent.

Streaker had switched to turbo-boost.

Streaker was homing in on Charlie like a cruise missile.

Streaker was jammed there like King Arthur's sword in the stone.

Streaker's ears streaming out behind her like jet-trails.

Text © 1996, Jeremy Strong.

No gains without pains

● The table below shows the different things that Trevor and Tina try, in order to make walking Streaker easier. Complete the table to show the outcome of each experiment and how it makes Trevor feel.

Trevor and Tina's experiments	Result	How does Trevor feel?
1. Being towed on roller-skates by Streaker		
2. Bribing Streaker with dog biscuits		
3. Communicating with Streaker via mobile phones		
4. Strapping a skateboard with a food bowl between two bikes for Streaker to follow		
5. Making an exercise bike-powered treadmill for Streaker		

● Which experiment successfully modifies Streaker's behaviour?

_____

● How and why does Streaker's behaviour change?

_____

Plot, character and setting

Storyboards

● Create a storyboard for a TV drama based on *The Hundred-Mile-An-Hour Dog*. Make notes on the main events and chapters involved in each episode. Above the text draw accompanying pictures. The first episode has been started.

Episode 1	Episode 2
Mum bribes Trevor to walk Streaker the dog. Trevor's roller-skate experiment is a disaster in market. (Chapters 1 and 2.)	
Episode 3	**Episode 4**
Episode 5	**Episode 6**

Talk about it

In someone else's shoes

Objective: To use some drama strategies to explore stories or issues.
What you need: Copies of *The Hundred-Mile-An-Hour Dog,* an enlarged copy of Extract 1 (page 8), access to an open space such as the hall, lightweight bags and a whistle.
Cross-curricular link: Drama.

What to do

● Tell the children that they are going to use drama to explore how Trevor feels. Read Extract 1 together, asking the children to imagine being pulled at great speed through a crowd, scattering shoppers, out of control. Underline the directional verbs: *zigzagged, careering, swerved.* Ask them to find a space and run about, demonstrating these verbs.
● Working in pairs, invite the children to take turns to role play the *mesmerized* old lady (holding a real bag on his/her arm) and Trevor (holding an imaginary lead). When you blow the whistle, those playing Trevor must head towards their partners, slipping the bag from their partner's arm as they pass, while the old lady actors act surprised and 'fall down'.
● Choose two to re-enact the scene with the rest of the class playing the crowd. Include dialogue.
● Discuss why each character deserves some sympathy.

Differentiation
For older/more confident learners: In groups of six to eight, choose another scene to dramatise, using dialogue from the text and/or improvising. Suggest Tina and Trevor's confrontation with Charlie.
For younger/less confident learners: For children taking speaking parts, provide the dialogue on cards. Encourage non-speakers to use face and body language.

Looks aren't everything!

Objective: To sustain conversation, explain or give reasons for their views.
What you need: Copies of *The Hundred-Mile-An-Hour Dog,* photocopiable page 22, writing materials and plastic mirrors.
Cross-curricular links: PSHE.

What to do

● Talk about how our different looks make us recognisable, but how others may not see us as we see ourselves.
● Read Chapter 3. Discuss how Trevor describes Tina and himself. Ask: *Why does Trevor mention Tina's freckles?* (They are distinctive.) Recall how Trevor does not understand why Tina dislikes them. Ask: *Do you think Tina sees Trevor as 'weedy'?*
● From Chapter 4, read Trevor's description of Charlie. Ask: *Is it flattering? Why not?* Discuss how much Trevor's feelings about Charlie influence his description.
● Hand out photocopiable page 22 and plastic mirrors. Ask the children to answer the questions and write a description of their own face.
● Bring the class together and invite individuals to describe one of their friends (without naming them), in a flattering way, but this time, only describing their personality. Can the others identify who it is? How does it compare with the person's written notes about themselves?

Differentiation
For older/more confident learners: Encourage the children to discuss how facial expressions (not the features themselves) influence others' opinions of our personality or mood.
For younger/less confident learners: Tell the children to experiment with pulling faces to depict different moods: angry, sad, surprised, shocked, and so on. Ask individuals to describe themselves and each other in the process.

Talk about it

Research and report

> **Objective:** To present information, with relevant details clearly sequenced and an effective ending.
> **What you need:** Copies of *The Hundred-Mile-An-Hour Dog*, writing material, access to the internet and encyclopedias.
> **Cross-curricular links:** Science, geography, history, art, ICT.

What to do

● Create a class list of the references that Trevor uses to describe Streaker and her speed. Divide the list by subheadings: natural phenomena (*whirlwind, mini-meteorite*), man-made devices (*torpedo, rocket, Exocet Missile*), fiction and film (*King Kong, King Arthur and his sword*).
● Arrange the class into seven groups. Allocate one of the above subjects (for example, whirlwinds or King Kong) to each group and ask them to research it (using the internet and books) and prepare a brief presentation for the rest of the class. They must make their report interesting, present facts in a logical order, and include an introduction and a closing statement or summary.
● Challenge the children to maximise their group talents, involving every child no matter what their strengths may be. Any children not presenting information might take notes or draw an illustration, diagram or other visual aid.

> **Differentiation**
> **For older/more confident learners:** Encourage research in greater depth, enabling a question-and-answer session at the end of the presentations.
> **For younger/less confident learners:** Provide the children with a list of useful websites and books. Help them to navigate sources of information, looking for key words, using an index.

Accusation and defence

> **Objective:** To create roles showing how behaviour can be interpreted from different viewpoints.
> **What you need:** Copies of *The Hundred-Mile-An-Hour Dog*, an enlarged copy of Extract 3 (page 10), photocopiable page 23 and writing materials.
> **Cross-curricular link:** Drama.

What to do

● Read Extract 3 together. Ask why Streaker is *under sentence of death*. Make a list of all the people Streaker has upset, including how and when.
● How can Trevor defend himself and Streaker? Discuss any extenuating circumstances that might justify their behaviour and lessen the seriousness of any offence. For example, in Chapter 7: the cat attacked first, the house-owners left the window open and they had tried knocking on the door.
● Recall how, in Chapter 10, Trevor wonders if there is a European Court of Doggy Rights. Imagine that there is. Hand out photocopiable page 23 and ask the children to discuss the evidence with a partner, first from Sergeant Smugg's point of view and then from Streaker's.
● Allocate the roles of Streaker's Defence and Accusation barristers to each pair, asking them to prepare a court case, based on their notes.
● Hold a class court, choosing one pair to role play opposing barristers. Invite them to call witnesses – the house owner, Sergeant Smugg, Dad – from members of the class. Have they decided on a verdict?

> **Differentiation**
> **For older/more confident learners:** Challenge one child to act as judge, to sum up the evidence for and against Streaker's survival. Ask the class jury to vote on the outcome of the court hearing.
> **For younger/less confident learners:** Concentrate on one episode only.

Talk about it

Exaggerations

> **Objective:** To actively include and respond to all members of the group.
> **What you need:** Copies of *The Hundred-Mile-An-Hour Dog* and photocopiable page 24 (copied onto card, cut into individual noun cards).

What to do

● Invite the children to share their favourite exaggerations used by Trevor, such as *my arms would have been stretched until they were about half a mile long.*

● Propose that these imply that Trevor has a vivid imagination. He draws on his awareness of the world to provide metaphors and comparisons. Explain that the children are going to play a game to stretch their imaginations.

● Arrange the children in a circle and invite each to pick a noun card (from photocopiable page 24) without looking first. Allow them a minute to think about their word. Take a card yourself to model how the game works.

● Explain that you will invite three questions about your word and that you will improvise your replies using exaggeration, sometimes with metaphor, simile and irony. For example, pick the word 'brick'. Suggest questions: *What is your brick like? Where did it come from? What is it for?* Improvise answers: *It's like a shoe box filled with lead; I bought it from Bricks R Us, the local builders' suppliers; I use it as a pillow to keep me awake when I mark your homework.*

> **Differentiation**
> **For older/more confident learners:** Invite the children to develop their object and responses into a paragraph of descriptive writing, or plot a short story.
> **For younger/less confident learners:** Allow children to share ideas. List question words or provide question cards to pick from a bag.

Ways and means

> **Objective:** To identify and discuss qualities of others' performance, including gesture and action.
> **What you need:** Copies of *The Hundred-Mile-An-Hour Dog,* dog-training manuals and internet access.
> **Cross-curricular links:** Drama, citizenship, ICT.

What to do

● Talk about why dog obedience is important, for the dog, the owner and the public. Recall Tina's phrase, *Behaviour Modification.* What is the more common term for teaching a dog obedience? (Training.)

● Ask the children, especially those who have dogs at home, how the characters' attempts to train Streaker are unconventional. Discuss why even bribery doesn't work. (Dog biscuits should reward achievement. Compare how Trevor's mum won't give him any money in advance of his success with Streaker.)

● Working in groups, ask the children to research conventional methods of dog training and to plan a dog-training demonstration. Suggest that they act out part of their presentation.

● Remind the groups that dogs don't learn everything at once. The children must plan a logical sequence to teach commands, starting by teaching the dog to respond to its name. (Ensure presentations retain audience interest.)

● Watch each group's performance and invite comments from the rest of the class on content, clarity and presentation quality. Identify what worked well and why.

> **Differentiation**
> **For older/more confident learners:** Ask the children to prepare a hint sheet or numbered instructions as a handout for owners wanting to train their dog.
> **For younger/less confident learners:** Invite in a responsible dog owner or local dog-trainer to give a talk on the subject before children prepare their own presentations. Also, provide a list of useful websites.

Talk about it

Looks aren't everything!

● Look at yourself in the mirror provided and answer these questions.

1. What is your most prominent (noticeable) feature?

_____

2. Which feature do you like best and why?

_____

3. What is your least favourite feature?

_____

4. Can you think of something that might make you feel more positive about your least favourite feature? (For example, one boy thought his eyebrows were too close together, until he decided they made him look like a clever inventor!)

_____

5. Imagine someone who has never met you is meeting you off a train. Write a short description of yourself to explain how they can recognise you.

_____

_____

_____

6. Pull a grumpy face. How has it changed your looks?

_____

7. Give a big smile. How do you look different now?

_____

8. In the book Trevor says he is the *Ideas Man* and Tina is the *Organizer*. What are you good at? What could you call yourself and why?

_____

_____

_____

READ & RESPOND: Activities based on The Hundred-Mile-An-Hour Dog

Accusation and defence

● Imagine that Streaker is going to the European Court of Doggy Rights to defend her behaviour. Consider the evidence, firstly from Sergeant Smugg's point of view (against Streaker), and then from Trevor and Streaker's point of view (for Streaker). Write notes in the spaces below. Weigh up the evidence and provide your verdict.

Evidence and opinions against Streaker

She's totally crazy. I'll have your dog destroyed.

Evidence and opinions in defence of Streaker

Summary (your own opinion)
I think Streaker should/should not [delete one] be destroyed because...

Illustrations © 1996, Nick Sharratt.

Talk about it

Exaggerations

● Copy this page onto card and cut out the individual noun cards to use in a word game.

boots	pillow	bike	rabbit	football
helmet	shell	cauliflower	coin	cake
clock	bag	wheel	piano	telephone
recorder	mug	wheelbarrow	mouse	umbrella
paintbrush	shed	brick	fishing net	teddy bear
face mask	hot-water bottle	apple	stilts	pot plant
feather	table lamp	camera	bucket	cage

Get writing

Same characters, new story

> **Objective:** To develop and refine ideas in writing using planning and problem-solving strategies.
> **What you need:** Copies of *The Hundred-Mile-An-Hour Dog* and writing materials.

What to do

● Read Chapter 3. Ask: *Why does Trevor say,* Mouse is very well trained? (Use of irony.) *Is Mouse any better trained than Streaker? Does he obey orders or is the St Bernard of a different nature from the greyhound? Which single order does he obey?* (Sit.) *Would any command have the same effect?* (Yes.)

● Create two lists of adjectives comparing and contrasting Streaker's and Mouse's natures, for example: Streaker – excitable, fast, unstoppable, wild, crazy, happy, bouncy, fearless; Mouse – quiet, slow, calm, unobtrusive, amiable, compliant, amenable.

● Recall the attempts to train Streaker and how success occurs by accident – inadvertently scaring the dog to avoid disobedience through association of a bad experience.

● In groups, discuss how Tina and Trevor could motivate Mouse to speed up and plan a storyline of how they encourage Mouse to race Streaker. This provides the broad plot, the children must plan the details and make it funny.

> **Differentiation**
> **For older/more confident learners:** Encourage each individual child to write their story in the style of Jeremy Strong, using humour, dialogue, irony, exaggeration and minimal description.
> **For younger/less confident learners:** Listen to the children's ideas and help them to storyboard their plot development before they begin to write. Display Extract 1 or 2 to model the punctuation and layout of paragraphs and dialogue.

Magical metaphors

> **Objective:** To show imagination through the language used to create emphasis and humour.
> **What you need:** Copies of *The Hundred-Mile-An-Hour Dog*, writing materials, photocopiable page 28 and thesauruses.

What to do

● Tell the children the following tale: one day when you got to the checkout at the supermarket and realised you had forgot your purse, your 'heart sank'. Discuss how this is a metaphor and compare the literal meaning of 'sank'. Invite a few individuals to recount an occasion when their heart sank.

● List and discuss similar metaphorical sayings: heavy hearted, butterflies in the stomach, between the devil and the deep-blue sea, blood ran cold, and so on.

● Ask the children to re-read the part in Chapter 7 where Trevor describes his feelings on discovering his father's mobile phone is broken: *my heart dive-bombed into my boots and hid there squealing with terror.* Ask: *Which verb replaces* sank *in this metaphorical phrase?* (Dive-bombed.) Talk about how adapting the simple metaphor and extending and exaggerating it makes it more dramatic and funnier.

● Hand out photocopiable page 28, and ask the children to use their imaginations as broadly and originally as they can, to create new, adapted and extended metaphors.

● Bring the class together to share their creative results.

> **Differentiation**
> **For older/more confident learners:** Challenge the children to incorporate one or two of their new metaphorical phrases into a short story.
> **For younger/less confident learners:** Provide thesauruses to help the children replace simple verbs with more exciting words.

Get writing

News headlines

Objective: To choose and combine words, images and other features for particular effects.
What you need: Copies of *The Hundred-Mile-An-Hour Dog*, Extracts 1 and 2 (pages 8 and 9), and writing materials.
Cross-curricular links: ICT, art and design.

What to do
● Display Extracts 1 and 2 and read them together. Suggest that a real-life event like either of these could end up as a headline in the local paper. Invite the children to suggest attention-grabbing headlines for the stories, such as 'Dog and Boy Crime Partners', 'Children Arrested as Fur Flies'. They could use also alliteration, for example 'Market Mayhem'. Make a list of the headlines.
● Discuss how crimes are reported in papers. Talk about use of language ('It is alleged…', 'First on the scene, Sergeant Smugg…') and exaggeration

or inaccuracy ('In a frenzied and unprovoked attack thieves smashed the window…').
● Ask the children to choose one of these events and read it again in *The Hundred-Mile-An-Hour Dog,* including the lead-up and consequence.
● Ask them to create a newspaper column, including direct quotations from those concerned, a 'photograph', and possibly a pull quote halfway through the report, picking out a gossipy or shocking piece of journalese.

Differentiation
For older/more confident learners: Let the children expand their news story and transfer it to a word-processing program, including drawings or digital photographs.
For younger/less confident learners: Act as scribe as the children suggest components for the report. Help them to sequence their ideas and use emotive language, cutting and pasting.

Dear diary

Objective: To write non-narrative text using structures of different text-types.
What you need: Copies of *The Hundred-Mile-An-Hour Dog,* photocopiable page 29, writing materials and scissors, if required.

What to do
● Talk about the genre and style of writing of the book (fiction; first person, past-tense narrative; in chapters) and the intended readership (children and young people with a sense of humour; animal lovers, perhaps).
● Ask the children if any of them keeps a diary. Discuss its function – to remember things, to create a journal of events and feelings, to mark appointments and reminders.
● Talk about who the intended readers of a diary are. (Usually just the writers themselves, unless they are famous.)
● Discuss the style of writing in a diary.

(Incomplete sentences; pronouns, especially 'I', may be missing; articles 'a', 'the' and even verbs may be missing.) The diarist might write simply: *To town on bus* meaning *I went into town on the bus,* or perhaps single words, such as *Cold* or *Bored.*
● Hand out photocopiable page 29. Explain that it is an imaginary diary entry, as might be written by one of the story characters. Ask the children to copy out the entries in the right order, adding a title to show whose diary it is. Can they work out which chapters these events occur in?

Differentiation
For older/more confident learners: Ask the children to write a diary entry for their favourite event in the book, written in the persona of another character.
For younger/less confident learners: Highlight the chapters the children need to re-read, then provide scissors for them to cut out the entries and physically arrange them in order.

Get writing

A ray of hope

> **Objective:** To use beginning, middle and end to write narratives in which events are sequenced logically and conflicts resolved.
> **What you need:** Copies of *The Hundred-Mile-An-Hour Dog,* writing materials, Extract 3 (page 10) and photocopiable page 30.
> **Cross-curricular link:** PSHE.

What to do

● Read Extract 3 together. Invite the children to summarise the content and mood of each paragraph. (First: presents the problem, with the whole family worried about the dog; second: shows how the family dealt with the problem short-term, but the problem persists; third: main character spots a *ray of hope* that could save the situation.)

● Underline the phrase *two days before the end of the holiday.* Talk about what purposes this serves. (Shows passage of time; reminds the reader that the problem is not just saving Streaker, but also assuring Trevor receives his £30 and avoids arrest and/or being plunged into a bath of dirty water.)

● Suggest that the extract has much in common with the balance of a whole story – it has a beginning (setting the scene/problem), a middle (actions on the way to the final outcome) and an ending (signs of success and a happy ending).

● Hand out photocopiable page 30 and ask the children to plan a story that includes a 'ray of hope'.

> **Differentiation**
> **For older/more confident learners:** Challenge the children to divide their story into short chapters, adding detail, and rewording if appropriate.
> **For younger/less confident learners:** Invite the children to work with a partner to share ideas and talk through plot development. Use Trevor and Tina as the main characters.

Inventions

> **Objective:** To use knowledge of phonics, morphology and etymology to spell new and unfamiliar words.
> **What you need:** Copies of *The Hundred-Mile-An-Hour Dog* and writing materials.

What to do

● Talk about what two things Trevor's mum does to lose weight and keep fit. (Eats low-calorie foods; works out on an exercise bike.)

● Did the children notice how the exercise bike gains a trade-name style word that describes what it does without any explanation needed? Can they find the name used halfway through Chapter 10? (*Exer-cycle.*)

● Ask: *Why is 'exer-cycle' a good name?* Invite the children to compare the missing part of the first word (-cise) with the word 'cycle'. What do they have in common? (A 'sigh' sound.) The two words dovetail to imply both exercise and cycling, derived from real words, retaining enough of the words to convey unambiguous meaning.

● Invite the children to invent names for each of the characters' inventions for exercising Streaker. Explain that they can use irony – for example, the roller-skate and dog-on-lead combo might be called a roll-wrecker.

● Ask the children to pick their favourite name and list other uses. These can be humorous. For example, the roll-wrecker could be useful for clearing fielders out of the way while scoring rounders in a game.

> **Differentiation**
> **For older/more confident learners:** Encourage the children to develop one of their ideas into another anecdote about Trevor and Streaker.
> **For younger/less confident learners:** Allow the children to work in small groups, sharing ideas, and closely re-reading scenes from *The Hundred-Mile-An-Hour Dog* to collect useful words to work with.

Magical metaphors

- Read the four simple metaphors below. Change the verb (shown in bold) and exaggerate and extend the metaphor to make it more dramatic and funnier.

- Here is an example of an exaggerated and extended metaphor from the book: '…my heart **dive-bombed** into my boots and **hid** there **squealing** with terror.'

I **upset** the apple cart. (I caused trouble.)

My head **was** in the clouds. (I was daydreaming of fanciful things.)

I **put** my foot in it. (I got into trouble by doing or saying the wrong thing.)

I was **caught** red-handed. (I was caught in the act of breaking the rules/law.)

- Choose one of your new extended metaphors above. Use it in a paragraph describing an awkward situation humorously. Write in the first person.

Text © 1996, Jeremy Strong.

READ & RESPOND: Activities based on The Hundred-Mile-An-Hour Dog

Get writing

Dear diary

- Read the five diary entries below. Whose diary do they belong to?
- Number each entry 1 to 5 and copy them in order.
- Finish the title to show whose diary it is.
- In which chapters of *The Hundred-Mile-An-Hour Dog* do these events occur?

Let Alsatians out by mistake (HA HA!) – chased Larkey's stupid dog.
Dad nabbed them for house-breaking. Top cop!
Collected bucket of frog spawn from ditch. (V. heavy. V. smelly.)
Poor Trevvy-Wevvy got knocked flying and nettled.
'Borrowed' trolley to carry Love Birds' Surprise to tin bath. Heh heh.

My Easter Holiday Diary by _____

1. _____

2. _____

3. _____

4. _____

5. _____

The events in this diary are based on what happens in

Chapters _____ and _____

Illustration © 2014, Simon Walmesley.

Get writing

A ray of hope

● Plan a story that includes a dramatic turning point which is the 'ray of hope' for the main characters. Decide how it will solve their problem.

My two main characters are:

1. _____   2. _____

● Use one idea from each section below to plot your story, or use your own ideas.

The main problem that the characters want to solve is:

☐ A pet is annoying the neighbours who want it put down or re-homed.	☐ One of the characters is being bullied on the way home from school.	☐ One character's birthday plans are ruined after their parent is made redundant.
☐ One character needs to learn to swim quickly to enjoy a special water-sports holiday.	☐ One character has to look after a new child in the class but they don't get on.	☐ One character's sports kit is stolen just before a competitive event.

☐ My own idea: _____

The ray of hope that leads to a solution to the problem is:

☐ The children spot an advert in the paper or the post-office window.	☐ The children find something in the street that is very valuable to someone else.	☐ A neighbour's parcel is mis-delivered to one character's address.
☐ The children go to a jumble sale and make a discovery.	☐ Somebody starts a local youth theatre group.	☐ There is a school outing to a theme park.

☐ My own idea: _____

● Write a summary of the plot: _____

_____

Assessment

Assessment advice

As the children read the book, observe their reactions and check for understanding of exaggeration and irony, two of the main components used to create humour out of this otherwise everyday situation and setting. What aspects of the story help them to empathise and identify with the characters? Observe if the children are able to guess the gist of any terms that are unfamiliar to them. For example, if they don't know what *Mach one* is, can they infer that it is an extreme speed that any animal is unlikely to reach?

When using any of the lesson plans, always close with a plenary session. Allow the children time to share their work and comment on their own and each other's achievements. Encourage individuals to assess their own efforts and results, from aspects that could be improved to areas in which they feel successful. Ask them to say what, if anything, they would do differently another time. Work on any areas where the children struggle by allowing extra time and/or teaching input.

Invite confident readers who enjoyed this book to read more novels by Jeremy Strong. Discuss these in groups, noting how far the children are able to identify similarities of style, content, characterisation and plot. Challenge them to write a book review saying what they liked about the story and its telling

Perspectives

> **Assessment focus:** To interrogate texts to deepen and clarify understanding and response.
> **What you need:** Copies of *The Hundred-Mile-An-Hour Dog*, photocopiable page 32 and writing materials.

What to do
● Ask the children if they enjoyed the story and why. Discuss how the author manages to make being bullied, getting into trouble, and even being arrested, funny.
● Ask the children to share examples of humour in the story, in terms of characterisation, plot and writing style, if possible giving direct quotations. For example, Trevor's image of himself as *the Ideas Man* is funny as most of his ideas end in disaster; having the fear of humiliation and unpleasant punishment at the hands of a bully adds a sub-plot to the main plot of attempts to train the dog and collect the reward.
● Look for examples of exaggeration and irony used by the narrator and share thoughts on how this adds to the humour of the storytelling, how it adds colour and focus, and how it indicates Trevor's personality and his light-hearted way of looking at life.
● Talk about the value of writing in the first person and of the protagonist having a friend with whom to share adventures and a safe haven of his home and family setting. Does it give readers confidence to laugh with the hero, as they know all will be well in the end?
● Provide each child with photocopiable page 32. Ask the children to find direct quotations from the text to support their responses to the questions, all of which share the same broad opening question: *How does the author make the story funny?*
● When the children have completed their photocopiable sheets, discuss their answers with them individually, to see how successfully they have expressed their thoughts. Then share responses as a class.

Assessment

Perspectives

● The setting for Jeremy Strong's *The Hundred-Mile-An-Hour Dog* is not unusual: an ordinary family with a loveable, energetic, but untrained dog. Answer the questions below about what makes the book funny, using direct quotations from the text.

How does the author make the situation funny...

...through characters' personalities, behaviour and relationships?
...through plot development and sub-plots?
...through use of language and style of writing?